DEVON
CUSTOMS
&
SUPERSTITIONS

COMPILED BY JAMES WHINRAY

TOR MARK PRESS · PENRYN

This book attempts to record many of the customs, cures and superstitions which were observed in Devon during Victorian times. Some of them, such as not walking under a ladder, survive across the whole of England even today, others were quite unknown outside Devonshire.

They include examples of bizarre beliefs, yet the greatest scientists of the seventeenth century, Newton and Hooke, experimented with folk remedies no less strange.
We forget how recent is modern medical knowledge.

Although we have drawn on many sources, three nine-teenth century writers preserved more than any others: Mrs Eliza Bray, Mrs HP Whitcombe, and Sarah Hewett. The Devonshire Association's *Transactions* are another major repository of the old folk-lore.

The Tor Mark series

Folklore

Classic Cornish ghost stories
Classic Devon ghost stories
Classic West Country ghost stories
Cornish fairies
Cornish folklore
Cornish legends
Customs and superstitions in
  Cornish folklore

Demons, ghosts and spectres in
  Cornish folklore
Devonshire customs and
  superstitions
Devonshire legends
The pixy book

Other titles

Charlestown
China clay
Classic Cornish anecdotes
Cornish fishing industry
Cornish mining – at surface
Cornish mining – underground
Cornish mining industry
Cornish recipes
Cornish saints
Cornwall in camera
Cornwall's early lifeboats
Cornwall's engine houses
Cornwall's railways
Devonshire jokes and stories
Do you know Cornwall?
Exploring Cornwall with your car
Harry Carter – Cornish smuggler
Houses, castles and gardens in
  Cornwall

Introducing Cornwall
King Arthur – man or myth?
Lost ports of Cornwall
Old Cornwall – in pictures
The pasty book
Shipwrecks around Land's End
Shipwrecks around the Lizard
Shipwrecks around Mounts Bay
Shipwrecks – Falmouth to Looe
South-east Cornwall
The story of Cornwall
The story of the Cornish language
The story of St Ives
The story of Truro Cathedral
Tales of the Cornish fishermen
Tales of the Cornish miners
Tales of the Cornish smugglers
Tales of the Cornish wreckers

First published 1996 by Tor Mark Press,
Islington Wharf, Penryn, Cornwall TR10 8AT
© 1996 Tor Mark Press
ISBN 0-85025-356-X
The cover illustration is by Ann Baum
Printed in Great Britain by Burstwick Print and Publicity Services, Hull

CUSTOMS ROUND THE YEAR

Valentine's Day

On this day a woman might choose who should be her Valentine, and tell him so. He was then obliged to present her with a pair of gloves – but in practice they were only given 'if there was a little sweet-hearting in the case'.

Shrove Tuesday

The farmers considered it a great holiday, and everybody who worked for them feasted on pancakes. The great sport of the day was to assemble round the fire and for each person to toss a pancake before he had it for his supper. The awkwardness of the tossers afforded great entertainment: they were compelled to eat their share even if it fell into the fire itself.

The other diversion for children was Lent crocking, when they went round the neighbourhood knocking on doors where a party was in progress and singing:

Lent crock, give a pancake,
Or a fritter for my labour,
Or a dish of flour, or a piece of bread,
Or what you please to render;
I see by the latch,
There's something to catch;
I see by the string,
There's a good dame within;
Trap, trapping throw,
Give me my mumps and I'll be go [gone].

If invited in, a cup of cider and a health followed. If not, the sport consisted in battering the house door with stones, because it was not open for hospitality. Then the assailant would run away, be chased and generally caught, and then had to undergo the traditional punishment – roasting the shoe. This consisted in an old shoe being hung up by the fire, which had to be kept in a constant whirl, roasting the culprit as well as the shoe, till some damsel had compassion on him and let him go; in this case he was expected to give her a little present at the next fair.

Mothering Sunday

This is not, as many imagine, a recent invention of greetings card manufacturers and florists, as the following description, from 1899, indicates:

In many parts of Devonshire and other western counties the

fourth Sunday in Lent is observed as a holiday under the title Mothering Sunday. Servants, apprentices and young working-folks in general visit their parents and between them make up very happy home parties. The previous Saturday is a busy day, for the mother is looking forward with great pleasure to the morrow's meetings and festivities. She busies herself in preparing the materials for a good dinner for the joyous youngsters, and gives them the very best she can afford. Of course, the mothering cake is her chief care. It is big and rich, and must be well baked, sugared and ornamented with fanciful designs. The dinner on Sunday consists of a hind quarter of lamb with mint sauce, a well-boiled suet pudding, sea kale, cauliflower, and wheat furmity with home-made wines. The day is one of mirthful enjoyment, mutual congratulations, and benevolence. The remains of the feast are usually distributed amongst needy neighbours who are unable to purchase these delicacies for themselves.

May Day

'Years since,' wrote Mrs Whitcombe in 1874, 'May-day was celebrated in the west of England with great festivities. Even the milkmaids would borrow articles of silver to hang upon their milk-pails, which were decorated with flowers and ribbons, and the prettiest girl in the village was the May Queen; but these customs have nearly all disappeared, except in some of the smaller places where a may-pole can still be seen.'

Sarah Hewett, writing in 1900, remarks that 'the old-fashioned demonstrations of mirth and hilarity have dwindled to feeble exhibitions of ill-dressed dolls, decked with wild flowers, carried in the hands of village children from house to house, where the occupants reward them with a few sweets or pence.'

Mrs Bray, in 1836, said that in her day the 'may-pole' sometimes joined in the procession, or even danced, for within a 'verdant pyramid crowned with flowers' was hidden a tall, strong man, and this character was known as 'Jack-in-the-Bush'. But by her time the hobby horse, once common throughout the West Country, was no longer in use. That custom is today preserved only at Padstow in Cornwall.

Ironically, there is probably more celebration of May-day now, with many primary schools having maypoles, than there was a century or more ago! Some customs, however, have fallen into disuse: May dew, collected before sunrise on May-day, was considered an infallible beautifier of the complexion; hawthorn bloom, gathered on the return from the fields, was hung over the porch to protect the inhabitants from witches and the evil eye; and on the first of May people were tricked into going on ridiculous errands, and when they returned empty-handed were derided as 'May guze-chicks' or 'May goslings' – antics now reserved for April Fool's Day.

Stinging nettle day

At Bovey Tracey on 3 May, all the children provided themselves with nettles and flogged each other.

Oak-apple, or Garland, Day (29 May)

Otherwise known as King Charles' Day, it commemorated the escape of Charles II after his defeat at the Battle of Worcester, by hiding in an oak tree – the source also of numerous Royal Oak pub signs.

Tiverton in particular celebrated the day until the early nineteenth century in a rough and boisterous fashion. At daybreak the church bells awakened the town with their clangour. Donning their oldest garments, the young men turned out and started to collect greenery from every available hedge and wood.

The fronts of public buildings, shops and houses were profusely decorated with branches of oak, from which were hung oak-apples previously decorated with silver paper. Every man wore an oak sprig and a small oak-apple in his button hole and his hat was garlanded with oak-leaves. Woe betide him who neglected these decorations!

Royalists (in smart clothes) and roundheads (dressed as scoundrelly ruffians) were led respectively by a regal King Charles and a repulsive Cromwell, naked to the waist, with a long shaggy tail made of several yards of hempen rope, which he used as a whip, and carrying a huge bag of soot.

The King's triumphant procession was completed by noon, when the two parties contrived to meet outside the Three Tuns Hotel. Now the battles began, with the soot liberally applied, and prisoners taken on both sides, until a general ransom at five o'clock when the festivities moved from the streets to the pubs. No women could venture out all day without danger. The evening's drinking was prolonged and heavy.

In other places the celebration was rather more restrained: the mock battle still took place, but the king's side were armed with kettles and pails of water, with which they drenched the republicans, but all in great good humour.

On the same day, small boys collected birds' eggs and begged flowers, which were then joined into garlands. The boys were fantastically dressed, with ribands round their arms and waist, and a smart garland cap upon their head, made of cardboard decorated with gold paper and little prints with a gilt border, intermixed with oak leaves. They paraded in groups, with the eldest boy carrying the garland, the others with whistles, drums, triangles and lath swords, collecting donations which they divided between them.

The hunting of the Earl of Rone

This curious ceremony was observed at Combe Martin on the north coast until it was suppressed in 1837. An Irish refugee calling himself 'the Earl of Tyrone' was supposed – by tradition if not by historians – to have been captured there in Tudor times.

A procession was formed of mummers, one representing the Earl wearing a grotesque mask, a smock-frock and twelve sea-biscuits strung around his neck; a hobby-horse masked and armed with a 'mapper' – an instrument shaped like a horse's mouth with teeth, and able to be snapped open and shut; a fool, masked; a donkey, also with a necklace of biscuits; and a troop of grenadiers armed with guns. On Ascension Day the grenadiers marched to Lady's Wood, near the village, and found the Earl of Rone hidden in the brushwood. They fired a volley, set him on the donkey with his face to the tail, and thus took him through the village to the sea, joined by the hobby-horse and the fool. At certain points the grenadiers fired and the Earl fell, mortally wounded. The spectators had to contribute to the drinks fund; if they did not, the hobby-horse laid hold of them with his teeth.

Crying the neck

Mrs Bray gives us a fine description of this custom in 1836.

One evening about the end of harvest I was riding out on my pony, attended by my servant who was born and bred a Devonian. We were passing near a field on the borders of Dartmoor, where the reapers were assembled. In a moment the pony started nearly from one side of the way to the other, so sudden came a shout from the field, which gave him this alarm. On my stopping to ask my servant what all the noise was about, he seemed surprised by the question, and said, 'It was only the people making their games, as they always did, to the spirit of the harvest.' I felt certain here was to be observed some curious vestige of an ancient superstition, and I soon gained all the information I could wish to obtain upon the subject.

When the reaping is finished, toward evening the labourers select some of the best ears of corn from the sheaves; these they tie together and it is called the nack. Sometimes, as it was when I witnessed the custom, this nack is decorated with flowers, twisted in with reed, which gives it a gay and fantastic appearance. The reapers then proceed to a high place, to 'holla the nack'. The man who bears this offering stands in the midst and elevates it whilst all the other labourers form themselves into a circle about him. Each holds aloft his hook and in a moment they all shout, as loud as they possibly can, these words, which I spell as I heard them pronounced:

'Arnack, arnack, arnack, wehaven, wehaven, wehaven.'

This is repeated three separate times, and the firkin is handed round between each shout by way of libation. When the weather is fine, different parties of reapers, each stationed on some height, may be heard from miles round, as it were in answer to each other.

The evening I witnessed the ceremony, many women and children, some carrying boughs and others having flowers in their caps or in their hands or in their bonnets, were seen, some dancing, others singing, whilst the men practised the rights in a ring. Can we for a moment doubt that this custom is a vestige of Druidism?

Mrs Bray, like many of her contemporaries, was obsessed with Druidism, and misinterpreted much of what she saw, yet there is little doubt that this ceremony is indeed of very ancient origin. Here are some variants of the cry recorded by other writers:

We ha'neck! We ha'neck!
Well a-plowed! Well a-sowed!
We've a-reaped! and we've a-mowed!
Hurrah! Hurrah! Hurrah!
Well a-cut, well a-bound!
Well a-zot upon the ground!
We ha'neck! We ha'neck!
Hurrah! Hurrah! Hurrah!

A-neck! a-neck! a-neck!
Whose neck?
Varmer Ferris'es! Varmer Ferris'es!
It's all a-cut!
It's all a-bound!
And all a-taken from the ground,
Hip! Hip! whorrah! whorrah!

After this the cider-firkin was passed around from mouth to mouth. Then a start was made for the farmer's kitchen, where a substantial amount of pork, beef, vegetables, figgy-pudden, cream, junkets, and gallons of cider awaited the hungry reapers, as well as the farmer's wife and his older children. When justice had been done to the food, long churchwarden pipes were produced, and more cider provoked merriment and indescribable tumult. Some recounted their experiences in winter, in snowstorms or floods, or their meetings with the Devil on lonely hills, or wanderings over swampy meadows in the footsteps of Jack-o'Lantern. Others sang the old songs, or songs they had themselves composed, and not until daylight streamed in did they seek their beds.

The neck was hung up over the kitchen table, and last year's neck was given to the best beast in the cow-shed.

Old Christmas Eve

Wassailing the apple trees is a custom which continued at least until the end of the nineteenth century, and was accompanied by a firm belief in the old verse, that

> More or less fruit they'll bring,
> As you do give them wassailing.

In the evening, the farmer's family and friends assembled, and, after partaking of cakes and cider, adjourned to the orchard, carrying with them a pitcher of the beverage and some cake. They hung pieces of this on the branches of one of the trees, and sprinkled the cider over its roots; then, forming themselves into a ring, they chanted:

> Here's to thee, old apple tree!
> Whence thou may'st bud and whence thou may'st blow,
> And whence thou may'st bear apples enow!
> Hats full! caps full!
> Bushel – bushel – sacks full!
> And my pockets full, too! Huzza!

This done, the farmer and his friends cheered several times, before leaving the orchard; it was also customary in some parts to fire guns at the apple-trees.

Christmas

The custom of burning the yule log is observed in large country houses at the present time [1900] on Christmas Eve, but where the fireplaces are contracted and slow combustion grates are the vogue, small branches of green ash are cut fresh from the plantation. These, sawn into lengths the width of the grate, are tied into faggots with four or five strong binds of bramble canes.

Very large faggots, such as are intended to be burnt in old-fashioned kitchen fireplaces, are bound with chains. The bramble binds are a source of much amusement, for soon after being placed on the dogs, they burn through, one by one. Before they begin to light and burn, each of the youngest members of the family chooses a bind, and whose is first burnt through will be the first to marry. It is customary for the company to drink a quart of cider at the bursting of each bind, so that by the time the whole have given way, there has been a large consumption of that beverage. It soon begins to influence the flow of spirits and induces a hilarious state of mind, increasing in strength as the night advances.

Giglet Fairs

At many towns and villages in Devon, on the first Saturday after Christmas and then again on Lady Day [25 March, until 1752 the official new year's day] it was customary for women and girls wishing to be hired as domestic servants to stand in rows on the 'fair-field' of each district. People who needed a servant would then make a tour of inspection, and agree terms for a year with an apparently suitable person. This custom continued until about the 1880s at Holsworthy, South Molton and Okehampton.

After the business of the day was over, a pleasure fair was held, known as the 'Giglet Fair'. The original meaning of giglet was 'a wanton wench'. At the Okehampton Giglet Fair, bachelors were allowed to approach girls without a formal introduction, not otherwise allowed in those straight-laced times when servants were not permitted 'followers'. Not infrequently, marriages followed soon after.

OTHER CUSTOMS

Blundell's School initiation

Blundell's School in Tiverton always prided itself on producing tough boys; they had to be able to fight, and they washed (or if reluctant were washed by their peers) at a pump in the yard. Such a school inevitably had rites of initiation – by water and by fire. New boys were stripped and thrown into Taunton Pool, to see whether they could swim. Then they were tied face-down to a bench and placed with their back to the fire. Every so often during the roasting process they were basted by a bucket of cold water being thrown over them. On one occasion, something more interesting occurred and the spit was left unattended, so the new boy died. After this the custom was mercifully stopped, though some old boys doubtless believed it marked the beginning of the end for the British Empire.

'Camp-le-tout, Newland'

According to Thomas Westcote, writing in 1630, foolish and provocative young men could try their luck in two villages just east of Barnstaple, then known as East and West Newland. They would shout out 'Camp-le-tout, Newland,' and attempt to escape the clutches of the good ladies of the village. Alas, our author does not explain the significance of this piece of colloquial French, or how it came about that the ladies of Newland understood it, but it is certain that they regarded it as such a slur on their collective chastity that they 'are instantly all up like a nest of wasps with the first alarm'. The streets were roped off and the culprit or culprits were beaten down from their horse with stones and similar missiles, which were always kept in readiness. The culprits were then 'washed, shaved and perfumed (and other like dainty trimming not for modesty to be spoken of) so that he that travels that way a fortnight after may smell what hath been done; and he that hath made the trial will confess by experience that it is folly for a wise man to anger a multitude causelessly.'

WAYS TO KNOW THE FUTURE

Born on a Sunday, a gentleman;
Monday fair in face;
Tuesday full of grace;
Wednesday, sour and glum;
Thursday, welcome home;
Friday, free in giving;
Saturday, work hard for your living.

But the more widely known version is

Monday's child is fair in face,
Tuesday's child is full of grace,
Wednesday's child is full of woe,
Thursday's child has far to go,
Friday's child is loving and giving,
Saturday's child works hard for its living;
And a child that's born on Christmas Day
Is fair and wise, good and gay.

Halloween nuts

On Halloween evening, clear the grate of all ashes, and ensure that the fire is burning brightly. Each girl present should set a large hazel nut upon the lowest bar, and sit in silence to await the result.

She whose nut first blazes, will be the first to marry.

She whose nut first cracks, will be jilted.

She whose nut first jumps, will soon start on a journey but will never marry.

She whose nut smoulders, will have sickness, disappointment in love, and perhaps die young.

Divination by water

Several young men and women should play simultaneously. They arrange for someone to place in the four corners of a room four bowls, one with clean water, the next with dirty water, the third with pebbles and the fourth empty. The 'players' are then blindfolded, led into the darkened room and placed back to back in the centre. All get onto their knees and crawl to any corner of the room, perhaps several going to one corner, feeling for the bowls.

Those who find the empty bowl may expect celibacy or poverty. The dish of clean water implies that the future spouse will never previously have married, whilst the dirty water implies a widow or widower as the future spouse. The dish of water with pebbles at the bottom implies a future of wealth and honour.

Bible divination

Choose a number between 3 and 27. Then open the Bible at Genesis chapter 49; read the verse whose number you chose. This will typify your fate, character, and success in life – provided you can understand the verse you have picked!

An alternative method, practised by country people throughout Britain on almost every occasion, was to open the Bible at random, point to a passage, and read a few words, which would throw light on the future, or the correct course of action.

Many people in Devonshire, if they had lost anything and suspected it to be stolen, took their front door key and tied it to a bible, placing it very carefully on Psalm 50, verse 18. ('When thou sawest a thief, then thou consentedst with him, and hast been a partaker with adulterers.') Two persons must then hold the book by the bow of the string attaching the key, first repeating the name of the suspected thief, and then the verse from the psalm. If the bible moves, the suspected person is considered guilty; if it does not move, then innocent.

Subjects of dreams

Ass: to dream one sees an ass labouring under a heavy burden indicates that the dreamer will, by hard work, amass a fortune.

Absent ones: to dream they are ill or in trouble shows they are in danger; if well, it is a sign that they are prosperous.

Angels: a happy dream, showing peace at home and a good understanding with your friends.

Baby: if you dream of holding a baby in your arms, it signifies trouble.

Bees: if you dream of a swarm of bees, you will be wise and respected. If they disturb or sting you, however, you will lose friends or even your sweetheart.

Carriage: if you dream that you are shut up in a carriage and cannot get out, it shows that false friends are slandering you, and you will suffer much at their hands.

Cats: Dreaming of cats shows that your female friends are treacherous.

Card playing: you will shortly be married.

Dancing: you will gain riches, honour and many friends. Your life will be long, happy and prosperous.

Dead: to dream of the dead brings news of the living.

Ducks in a pond: an omen of good luck.

Eggs: if you are eating eggs in a dream, you will be delivered from great tribulation; but to break them raw shows loss of friends and fortune.

Empty vessels: your life will be one of toil and privation.

Eating: portends sickness and death.

Fish: to dream of fish shows that you will have abundance of wealth and good things. Also that you will be successful in love.

Fire: you will have hasty news.

Flowers: always a good dream, a sure sign of joy, success and prosperity.

Garden: to dream of being in a beautiful garden shows you will be rich and prosperous in love.

Broken glass: quarrels and family strife.

Hares: great trouble in pecuniary matters and sickness.

Horses: your life will be long and happy; but if kicked by a horse in a dream, you will have a long and severe illness, or other misfortune.

Ivy: your friendships are true.

Inn: a very favourable dream – you will inherit a large fortune, be successful in all your undertakings and will enjoy much happiness.

Jackdaw: beware of danger from evil people.

Journey: to be about to take a journey means you will soon have a reversal of fortune.

Knives: always omens of evil about to happen.

Kiss: to dream that some one is kissing you is a sure sign that you are being deceived. To dream that you are kissing some one whom you love is a sign that your love is not reciprocated.

Larks: a good sign – you will overcome all difficulties that may come in your way, and will speedily rise to a good position.

Lightning: if without thunder, this is one of the very luckiest dreams. To lovers it means, happiness; to farmers, good crops; to sailors, prosperous voyages.

Magpies: you will soon be married.

Nightingales singing: bright days are coming, and a release from all anxieties.

Nuts: indicate the receipt of money.

Oats: an omen of success.

Onions: you will find much money.

Parcel: to be carrying a parcel indicates you will receive a letter from abroad.

Quarrels: to dream of them is a sign that you will soon be profitably engaged in a business matter.

Rain: an omen of misfortune.

Rats: enemies are near at hand.

Teeth: a dream about teeth is the unluckiest of all dreams. If a tooth falls out, it signifies sickness; if all your teeth drop from the gums, then death.

Ships: if they are sailing in clear waters it is a favourable omen, but if the water is murky, then most unfavourable.

Silver coins: if you pick them up (unless they are mixed with gold) you are going to be short of money.

Ugliness: if you see yourself reflected as ugly, it is an omen of success.

Umbrella: to lose one in a dream signifies a business loss.

Valentine: to dream of receiving one is a bad sign – illness and trouble will soon be upon you.

Violin: to dream of playing a violin denotes a forthcoming marriage – unless a string breaks, when you will not marry at all.

Water: clear water means you will get good news, murky water bad news.

Wedding: to dream of a wedding portends a funeral.

Yachting: in clear water on a sunny day, this is prophetic of great happiness.

Yew trees: you will hear of the death of an aged person in whom you have a pecuniary interest.

FORETELLING YOUR MATE

Hempseed sowing

One of the most widespread superstitions was that, by 'sowing' hempseed at a certain time of year (variously, St Valentine's Eve, Midsummer and Halloween), a girl could see her future husband. On St Valentine's Eve girls went to the church-porch with hempseed in their hands, and, as the clock struck twelve, started towards home, casting the hempseed as though they were sowing a crop, and expecting to see their future partners following them. The action had to be accompanied by these words:

> Hempseed I sow,
> Hempseed I mow
> He that will my true love be,
> Come rake this hempseed after me.

The Midsummer sowing of hempseed was similar, but at Halloween the custom was suitably scary, even though it could be done at home – and was probably less widespread. The front door had to be left securely open, so that it could not be shut by accident. As midnight struck, the girls would rush, each in a different direction, sowing the seed and calling:

> Hempseed I sow,
> Hempseed I throw,
> He that's my true-love
> Come after me and mow!

The spirits of the future lovers were expected to be beyond the shrubs ready to rush after the sowers, and unhappy would be the maiden who could not get over the threshold before the scythe of the spirit reaper caught her.

Leaden letters

A young man could find the initials of his bride by melting some lead and dropping it into a bowl of water, when it would set into the initials of his future wife.

Yarrow

In many villages, girls would pluck yarrow from a man's grave, in the belief that if they placed the yarrow under their pillow and repeated the following, their lovers would appear to them in a dream:

> Yarrow, sweet yarrow, the first that I have found;
> And in the name of Jesus I pluck it from the ground.
> As Joseph loved sweet Mary and took her for his dear,
> So, in a dream this night, I hope my true love will appear.

Midsummer Eve

In addition to sowing hempseed on this day, a girl might use other magic. On retiring to rest, she could place her shoes in the form of the letter T, and repeat:

> I place my shoes like a letter T,
> In hopes my true love I shall see,
> In his apparel and his array,
> As he is now and every day.

The shoes are reversed and these lines are said three times. Then she could write letters of the alphabet on pieces of paper, throw them face downward into a basin of water, and put the basin under her bed. In the morning she would look anxiously to see if any of the letters had turned over, face upwards; if so, the initials visible indicated the name of her future husband.

Pluck a rose on Midsummer Day, put it away and do not look at it, and it will be found as fresh on Christmas Day as when it was gathered; then wear it at church, and the intended partner will come and take it from you.

The first new moon after Midsummer was often greeted with these words:

> All hail, new moon, all hail to thee!
> I pray to thee, new moon,
> Before thou growest old,
> To reveal unto me
> Who my true love shall be!

Many of the old country folk would have assured you that, on seeing the first new moon in the year, if you take a stocking off one foot and run across a field, you will find a hair between the great toe and the next, which will be the colour of your lover's.

Some say that the new moon is not necessary. Simply perform the following rite. Retire to bed just before midnight, as quietly as possible. Remove the left garter, and tie it round the right stocking, repeating the following:

> This knot I knit,
> To know the thing I know not yet;
> That I may see
> The man who shall my husband be,
> How he goes and what he wears
> And what he does all days and years.

During the night the future 'he' will appear, in his everyday clothes, carrying something indicative of his trade or profession.

To discover the initials of your future husband

28 October, the day dedicated to Saints Simeon and Jude, is the most propitious for the following charm. Take a fine round apple and peel it in one single length. Take this paring in the right hand, stand in the centre of a large room, and while waving the paring gently around your head repeat:

> St Simeon and St Jude, on you I intrude,
> By this paring I hold to discover.
> Without delay, tell me I pray,
> The first letters of my own true lover.

Then drop the paring over the left shoulder and it will form the initial of your future husband's name; but if it breaks into small pieces, you will die an old maid.

The ash and the clover

An even leaved ash and a four leafed clover are excellent attractors of the opposite sex. A woman who finds an even-leaved ash can hold it flat in both hands, and repeat softly,

> With this even leaved ash between my hands
> The first I meet will be my dear man.

And then placing it in the palm of the gloved right hand, she should say

> This placed in my glove
> Will bring my true love.

and then remove it to the bosom and whisper,

> This even leaved ash in my bosom
> Will give me, in the first man I meet,
> My true husband.

To discover if one will ever marry

On Christmas Eve go into the yard and tap smartly at the door of the hen-house. If a hen first cackles, you will never marry, but if a cock crows first, then you will marry before twelve months are past.

MARRIAGE

Which day of the week?

> Monday for wealth,
> Tuesday for health,
> Wednesday is the best day of all;
> Thursday for crosses,
> Friday for losses,
> Saturday no luck at all.

Sunday is an exceptionally fortunate day to enter the holy state. (The present almost universal custom of marrying on Saturdays is clearly at the root of the rising divorce rate.)

Ensuring happiness

Pelting the lucky pair with rice as they leave the church, and throwing old slippers at them as they leave for their honeymoon are both traditional, but wedding guests in Devonshire should also carry sprigs of rue and rosemary, and a few cloves of garlic in their pockets or in their bouquets, to enhance the felicity of the couple. The bride should carry a small packet of bread and cheese in her pocket to give to the first woman or girl she meets after leaving the church. A bag of nuts should be presented to the groom within the church porch.

Wedding omens

Terrible misfortunes will follow if a raven should hover over the couple's path, or if they allow a cat, dog or hare to pass between them, or if they encounter a toad, frog or reptile. These creatures can easily be the embodiment of a witch, a pixy, or some evil spirit; even his satanic majesty may assume the form of an animal, to enable him to work ill fortune into their future lives at this time, when the couple are peculiarly open to benign or baleful influence.

On the other hand, 'Happy is the bride that the sun shines on.'

Chaining the bride

A peculiar wedding custom was observed at Lynton, where the bride was chained to the gates of the churchyard. Young men stretched rope, or chains of twisted straw and hay, decorated with ribbons and flowers, across the gate of the churchyard effectually preventing the exit of the bridal party. The bridegroom then scattered handfuls of small coins on the ground, and the chain was dropped, allowing their departure.

DEATH OMENS

The robin, especially if by ill chance it should enter a room, portends death very soon in the household. An educated lady gave this account in 1891:

In 1848 I was staying with my grandparents in Ashburton. My grandmother, having a severe cold, went early to bed, and the weather being oppressively hot, the window was left open. Presently a robin, dishevelled and melancholy, flew into the room and perched on the towel-rail. No amount of persuasion could dislodge him, and at last all efforts to eject him were abandoned. He continued his sad weep, – weep, – weep, – for at least an hour, when he quietly flew out of the window. That night, grannie died. Again, in 1851, a robin, just as unhappy and forlorn as the former one, flew into my father's bedroom, exhibiting every sign of dejection. Nor could he be easily driven off, but sought the tester of the bed, where he continued his weep, – weep, – weep. That night my father died.

Again, in the autumn of 1884, while on a visit to Dawlish with my husband and children, we often took our books and work into the garden. One evening, as usual, we were in the summerhouse, the children playing noisily, when a robin flew into their midst and hopped onto the table, finally perching himself on the handle of my work-basket. A more pitiable dejected little birdie could not be imagined, his feathers were ruffled and towsled, and both wings drooped to his feet. There he sat, uttering his dolorous weep, – weep, – weep, – for several minutes; when we rose to go into the house he followed, sometimes fluttering along before us in the path, at others flitting from bush to bush close at our side. Even after we had closed the window we heard him on the shrubs outside, still pathetically uttering his weep, – weep, – weep. The next morning my dear husband, who had gone along the Strand for a stroll while I dressed the children for a walk, dropped suddenly dead and was brought home within a quarter of an hour of leaving the house. Can you wonder at my having a dread of a visit from a robin?

If a corpse retained heat and flexibility, it was said that others of the same family would die before the year is out.

If letters crossed in the post, it was a sign of death.

If a tablecloth was returned from the laundry with a diagonal fold, that also was a sign of an impending death.

Certain families had their own omens of death, and some places had a general ability to predict. For example at North Tawton there was a house, in front of which was a pit; this was usually dry, but occasionally in a dry spell it would suddenly fill with water, and this always foretold the death of some great person. In the Oxenham family, a white throated-bird frequently appeared just before the death of a member.

Customs associated with death and funerals

When a person was dying, their departure could be made less painful by ensuring that all the locks and bolts in the house were unfastened, that there was no beam above their head, and that the bedding was not made of goose feathers.

It was vital to inform the bees of the death of a relative, by tapping at each hive with the key of the front door, saying as one tapped, 'Maister is dead,' or 'Missus is dead,' as the case might be. The bees were placed in mourning, by placing a black crape or cloth on the top of each hive. On the day of the funeral, any beehives which had belonged to the deceased were to be turned round.

After a death in the family, the pot plants should also be put in mourning with black crape ribands, otherwise they will die too.

A bottle should be put on the window sill of the room in which a corpse lies, 'to catch the angels' tears'; it should be left there forty days and forty nights.

LUCKY TIMES AND LUCKY OMENS

Tuesday and Wednesday are lucky days; Thursday has one lucky hour – the hour before sunrise.

The first wish on perceiving a shooting star will be granted. It is unlucky to see the new moon over the left shoulder or through glass; over the right shoulder (provided you are out of doors) is a happy omen, and straight before you indicates good fortune until the end of the moon. If you first see the moon over your right shoulder, you should shake your pockets, and pull out your money to let the moon shine on it.

On first hearing the cuckoo in spring, even before you write to the *Times* you should run in a circle three times with the sun, to ensure good luck for the rest of the year. If you first hear it to your right, it portends good fortune, but to hear it first on the left hand is a sign of impending ill-fortune.

If you first hear the cuckoo in April, run as fast as possible to the nearest gate, and sit on the top bar to drive away the spirit of laziness. Whoever neglects to do this will be weak-willed for a year, and have no inclination to work until the next spring.

On Good Friday it is lucky:

To break a piece of pottery.
To wean a child.
To sow all kinds of garden seeds: beans and peas in particular yield better crops.
To plant ornamental shrubs.

The following things are lucky

To stumble while ascending stairs, steps or ladders.

To find a cast horse-shoe in the road.

To see a pin and pick it up.

To carry crooked coins in the pocket.

To see fairies dancing at the entrance to a mine, which indicates valuable lodes.

To pay your bills on the first of January, which ensures you will have ready money throughout the year to pay future bills.

To spit over the right shoulder when you meet a grey horse.

To meet a flock of sheep on the highway.

To throw a pinch of salt into the mash when brewing, to keep the witches out.

To rest bars of iron on vessels containing beer in summer, which prevents souring of the beer in thundery weather.

To have crickets in the house.

To see a star on the wick of a candle.

To carry a badger's tooth in the waistcoat pocket (it brings luck at cards).

To have white specks on one's finger nails, which shows happiness is in store: these spots are sometimes called 'gifts'.

To be born on a Sunday, because you can see spirits and tame the dragon which watches over buried treasure.

To bite a baby's nails rather than cutting them, until it is a year old, because this will make it honest throughout life.

The put the left stocking on first.

To extend the right foot first when you start walking.

To fell trees only when the moon is waning and the wind is in the north.

To be the seventh son of a seventh son.

Business practice

When you have started any new business, the first cash taken should be turned over from hand to hand and spat upon to ensure good luck in future dealings.

When a bargain was struck for the sale of a cow or horse, it was customary for the seller to give a small token – a penny, or sometimes a shilling – back to the buyer as 'luck money'. The origin of the custom is unknown.

The last load of harvest

This last cart should be driven out of the field by a woman. If she avoids hitting the gatepost, she shall remain 'missus of the hayfield' for a further year.

BAD LUCK

Evil days

Whoever washes clothes on Good Friday will wash one of their family away, who will die before the year is out.

No new enterprise should be started on any of the following:

January 3rd, 4th, 5th, 9th 11th	February 13th, 17th, 19th
March 13th, 15th, 16th	April 5th, 14th
May 8th, 14th	June 6th
July 16th, 19th	August 8th, 16th
September 1st, 15th, 16th	October 16th
November 15th, 16th	December 6th, 7th, 11th

It is unlucky

To keep evergreens which have been used for the Christmas decorations until Candlemas Day [2 February]. Should a branch be found after that day, it is significant of impending death.

To have an empty pocket (even a crooked coin keeps the devil away).

To buy a broom in May, for it sweeps all luck away.

To wash your hands in the same water as another person: you will quarrel with them shortly.

To pass under a ladder without first crossing the middle fingers over the index fingers. (This widespread superstition is sometimes said to have arisen from the gallows at Tyburn, where the victim climbed a ladder which was then knocked away.)

To break a salt cellar.

To spill salt at table, without throwing a pinch over the left shoulder.

To help another person to salt, or to be helped.

To kill a robin or a cricket or a swallow.

To bring a single daffodil into a house; new-laid eggs will addle.

To neglect to communicate any great social or political event to the bees.

To sell a beehive: it should be bartered for a sack of wheat.

To move a hive, except on Good Friday.

To hear the cuckoo first upon your left hand.

To give a friend a knife, as it cuts away all friendship. (Charge them a penny for it.)

To turn a feather bed or cut one's nails on a Sunday.

To begin to do anything on a Friday; to start a journey or make a bargain on that day will prove disastrous.

To sow seed during the first three days in March, which were formerly called 'blind days'.

To speak while the clock is striking.

To put a pair of boots or an umbrella on the table.

To stir the leaves in a teapot before pouring out the tea.

To have a kitten and a baby in the house together; the baby will be unhealthy.

To cross knives.

To pass another person on a staircase.

To break a looking glass, which brings seven years bad luck or the loss of one's best friend.

To kill a small red spider, because this 'money-spider' brings money in its track.

To sneeze before breakfast.

To begin a new undertaking, or move house, on a Friday.

To return, or look back at the house, when starting a journey, or even a short walk. If compelled to return, one should sit and wait a few minutes before starting out again.

To eat any kind of fish from the head downwards.

To whistle while underground, because it will awaken the evil spirits which haunt caves and mines.

To whistle at sea, as it raises storms.

To be born with a blue vein across the nose.

To decorate a house with peacocks' feathers.

To meet a snail when entering a mine.

To see one magpie alone, which implies sorrow, or four which presages death. (If you do see one magpie, you should bow low to it.)

To reveal a child's Christian name before it is presented at the font for baptism.

To burn bones, as this will bring pains and aches.

To hear a cock crow at midnight, or a dog to howl between sunset and sunrise.

To see a pin and let it lie: you'll need that and hundreds more before you die.

To be born in May. Kittens born in May (May-chats, as they were termed in Devon) were immediately drowned by the superstitious, as to keep one would inevitably bring sorrow to the house.

To look into a mirror at dusk or nighttime, unless the room is well lit; there is always the prospect of seeing something nasty peeping over your shoulder, which would portend death.

To bring into a poultry farmer's house a small bunch of primroses, because this will limit the number of birds reared to the number of primroses. Better let them lie on the bank.

To hear the ticking of the death watch beetle.

To see a raven hovering over a house – very ominous for its inhabitants.

To transplant parsley.

To sit down at table as one of thirteen.

To lose a mop or broom at sea.

To plant lilies-of-the-valley – it would bring a death within a twelvemonth.

It is unlucky

For rooks to desert their rookery without any apparent reason, which forebodes ill-luck to the owners of the property.

For a child not to cry when baptized. The more it yells and screams, the faster the evil spirits will quit it.

For an unmarried person to be a sponsor at a baptism.

For one's nose to itch, for then one will be kissed, cursed, vexed or shake hands with a fool. To avert the three former ills, the remedy is to shake hands with a friend – which seems rather hard on the friend since they are presumably the fool!

For a visitor to enter a house and not sit down.

When losing at cards, you should rise from your chair and twist it round on one of its legs four times, which will improve your luck.

If your right ear burns, your friends are talking kindly of you, but if the left ear burns, they are 'picking holes in your jacket'. Let left or right burn at night, then all things are well, both in and out of sight.

Fishermen's superstitions

Never mention rabbits, hares or pigs while aboard, nor lend anything from one boat to another. Avoid turning the boat anti-clockwise.

If the first herring of the season is a 'melt' (that is, a male) then a disastrous time in the fishing world is to be expected; if a 'roe' (female) then it will be a profitable season.

Never throw a cat overboard or allow one to drown at sea.

CHARMS

To counter the evil of seeing birds of ill omen

Clean birds by sevens,
Unclean birds by twos,
The Dove in the heavens
Is the bird which I choose.   (Repeat seven times.)

To protect yourself against thieves and enemies

In the power of God I walk on my way.
In the meekness of Christ, what thieves soe'er I meet
The Holy Ghost to-day shall me keep.
Whether I sit or stand, walk or sleep,
The shining of the sun
Also the brightness of his beams shall me help.
The faith of Isaac to-day shall me lead;
The sufferings of Jacob to-day be my speed.
The devotion of the holy Lamb thieves shall let,
The strength of Jesus's passion them beset,
The dread of death hold thieves low,
The wisdom of Solomon cause their overthrow.
The sufferings of Job set them in hold,
The chastity of Daniel let what they would.
The speech of Isaac their speech shall spill,
The languishing faith of Jerome let them of their will.
The flaming fires of hell to hit them I bequeath,
The deepness of the deep sea their hearts to grieve.
The help of Heaven cause thieves to stand.
He that made the sun and moon bind them with his hand
So sure as St Bartholomew bound the fiend,
With the hair of his beard.
With these three sacred names of God known and unknown:
Miser, Sue, Tetragrammaton, Christ Jesus!
                    Amen

['Tetragrammaton' is not gibberish. The ancient Hebrew name
for God, Yahweh, could not be spoken, and was usually written
YHWH. 'Tetragrammaton' means 'a four-letter-word', and in
mystic writings of the seventeenth century was indeed used as
a name of God. 'Miser Sue' is presumably a corruption of church
Latin, but has not been identified.]

Charm used when gathering herbs for magical purposes:

Hail to thee, holy herb,
Growing on the ground.
All on Mount Calvary
First was thou found.
Thou art good for many sores,
And healeth many a wound;
In the name of St Jesu!
I take thee from the ground.

To murder one of the family

Sew into one of their undergarments a long, thin, herring bone. As the bone dries up, or withers, so will the person wearing it gradually pine away and die.

To know if one's fiancé will be true

Procure from the butcher, or the cook, the bladebone of a shoulder of lamb. Borrow a penknife from an unmarried man, but do not say for what purpose it is required. Take a yard of white ribbon, and having tied it to the bone, hang it as high in your bedroom chimney as you can conveniently reach. On going to bed, pierce the bone with the knife once, for nine successive nights, in a different place each night, repeating as you do so:

> 'Tiz not this bone I means to stick,
> But my lover's heart I means to prick,
> Wishing him neither rest nor sleep
> Till unto me he comes to speak.

At the end of the nine days your sweetheart will ask you to bind a wounded finger, or attend to a cut which he will have met with during the time the charm was being used.

To make cows yield more milk and preserve them from disease

Collect straw, pile it in a heap on a large flat stone and light it, then force the cows to pass over the dying embers.

To recover lost money

A 'white witch' professed to be able to restore a lost sum of money with the following incantation:

> Flibberty, gibberty, flasky flum,
> Calafac, tarada, lara, wagra wum,
> Hooky, maroosky, whatever's the sum,
> Heigho! Presto! Money come!
> In the name of the Father, Son and Holy Ghost.   Amen

To secure luck at games of chance

Suspend by a silken cord around the neck, a section of the rope with which a person has been hanged.

To charm away house flies

Gather and dry as much of the herb fleabane as you can find. Each morning during the months of June, July and August, burn a handful of the herb in the rooms. This smoke will drive the flies from the house.

To prevent fleas from entering a house

When you first hear the cuckoo in spring, take some of the earth from the place where your right foot is standing and sprinkle it on the threshold of your front door; but speak of it to no one. Neither fleas, beetles, earwigs or vermin of any other sort will cross it.

To dispel the vapours

St John's wort, or Devil's flight, gathered on St John's Day or on a Friday, dried and placed in a closely covered jar and hung in a window, will protect the house from thunderbolts, storms, fire and evil spirits.

If the flowers and leaves are dried and ground into powder and then placed in a silken bag and hung round the neck, the wearer will be successful in love, and be cured of the vapours and all other mental afflictions. To ensure absolute immunity from these ills, however, it is necessary to operate in July, on the evening of the full moon.

To bring milk to butter

Come, butter, come,
Come, butter, come,
Peter's waiting at the gate,
Waiting for a buttered cake,
Come, butter, come.

To frustrate the power of a black witch

Take a cast horseshoe and nail it above your door, points upward. While nailing it chant, in a monotone:

So as the fire do melt the wax
And wind blows smoke away,
So in the presence of the Lord
The wicked shall decay,
The wicked shall decay. Amen

To destroy the power of a witch

Take three small-necked stone jars; place in each the liver of a frog stuck full of new pins, and the heart of a toad stuck full of thorns from the holy thorn bush. Cork and seal each jar. Bury in three different churchyard paths, seven inches from the surface and seven feet from the porch. While burying the jars, repeat the Lord's prayer backwards.

As the hearts and livers decay, so will the witch's power vanish. After performing this ceremony, the operator can never again be subject to the power of any witch.

Baptismal water

This was considered useful in magical rites, which is why fonts used regularly to be kept locked. It was also unlucky to baptise more than one child in the water; the last child would pick up all the sins of those who had earlier been baptised, so a fresh supply was needed for each baptism.

CURES

For thrush

Procure three rushes from a clear stream; pass them separately through the mouth of the infant; throw them into the water, and, as the current bears them away, so will the complaint disappear.

Or alternatively:
Catch a duck and place its mouth, wide open, within that of the child, and, as the sufferer inhales the duck's breath, the complaint will leave it.

Or again
Read Psalm VIII over the head of the infant three times, three days in a week, in three successive weeks.

For a woman with fits

Attend a church service with thirty young men; sit in the church porch after the service, and let each of the young men, as they leave the church, drop a penny into your lap, until the thirtieth comes, and he should take up the 29 pence and substitute a half-crown [a coin worth 2s.6d. or 30 pence]. With this coin in your hand you should walk three times round the communion table, and afterwards have the half-crown made into a ring, by which means you shall recover your health.

Or alternatively
Take a jay, pluck and clean it and roast to a cinder. Pound it up in a mortar and add a teaspoonful every morning to the first cup of tea of the day.

To cure the King's Evil

This cure is very similar to that for fits. A relative of the patient, but of the opposite sex, takes the collection, on the right hand side of the church porch. Once the pennies have been exchanged, the centre of the half-crown is cut out, and the outer ring is suspended round the neck of the afflicted person. The centre piece is reserved until the next funeral takes place, when it is dropped into the grave just before the coffin is lowered in.

Letter to the Vicar of Tavistock, 1835

Rev. Sir,

I should take it as a great favour if your Honour would be good enough to let me have the key of the churchyard tonight, to go in at twelve o'clock, to cut off three bits of lead about the size of a half-farthing, from three different shuts [water-spouts], for the cure of fits.

Sir, I remain,

Your obliged, humble servant ....

For a child with a rupture

Split an ash tree and wedge the hole open with two large timbers. Then three people should take the sufferer to the tree at daybreak and pass him through the tree three times, clockwise. Take out the wedges and bandage the tree. As the tree heals, so will the sufferer.

For sores and wounds

Images stolen from a church font and ground down to powder may be applied externally for wounds and sores, or drunk in solution for internal complaints. Apostles are better than other saints (although St Peter is the best of all), and any saint is better than a gargoyle, but all will have some effect.

For ague

Visit at dead of night the nearest cross-roads on five different occasions, and at the point where the roads meet, bury a new-laid egg; this must be done about an hour before the attack is expected; as the patient buries the egg, the ague will be buried also.

To cure inflammation

Scour the inflamed part with strong brine, then wash with soap and plenty of hot water, Eat much raw beef for several days.

To cure fits

Wear a ring, fashioned from three nails or screws which have been used to fasten a coffin, and dug up out of the churchyard.

To prevent toothache

Carry an old tooth in the pocket which has been bitten from a skull found in a churchyard. Failing this, any dead person's tooth, carried in the left waistcoat pocket, may be of some use.

For a wen on the neck

Rub the neck three times each way on each side of a newly dug grave.

To cure skin disease

Place the poison found in a toad's head in a leathern bag one inch square; enclose this in a white silk bag and tie it round the neck, allowing the bag to rest on the pit of the patient's stomach. On the third day the patient will be sick. Remove and bury the bag. As it rots, so will the patient get well.

To remove warts

Take an eel and cut off the head. Rub the warts with the blood of the head. Then bury the head in the ground. When the head is rotten, the warts will fall off.

Or alternatively:

Take as many pebbles from a running stream as you have warts, tie them tightly in a clean white bag and throw them into the highway or street. Then wash each wart in vinegar seven successive mornings. (Anyone who picks up the bag will unfortunately get the warts transferred to them, but that's not your problem.)

To cure diarrhoea

Take a stale hot cross bun and place it in a hot oven to dry. Grate it into powder. When required, mix with cold water and take as a medicine. [Ingredients for many folk remedies, such as powdered turkey rhubarb, toads' livers and clean river water are now hard to obtain. Hot cross buns however – once associated with Good Friday – are these days available in supermarkets at most seasons of the year, so this particular remedy may now be more easily produced than in the nineteenth century.]

Mouth wash for toothache

Two quarts of rat's broth, one ounce of camphor and one ounce of essence of cloves, mixed together.

To prevent toothache

Cut your toe and finger nails and wrap the parings in tissue paper; insert the packet into a slit made in the bark of an ash tee before sunrise. You should never get toothache again.

To assist children in teething

Make a necklace of beads cut from the root of henbane, and place round the child's neck.

Charm for a bruise

Holy chicha! Holy chicha!
This bruise will get well by and by.
Up sun high!
Down moon low!
This bruise will be quite well very soon!
In the name of the Father, Son and Holy Ghost.   Amen.

To cure colic

Mix equal quantities of elixir of toads and powdered Turkey rhubarb. The dose is half a teaspoonful on an empty stomach for three successive mornings.

Charm to staunch blood

Jesus was born in Bethlehem,
Baptized in the River Jordan, when
The water was wild in the wood,
The person was just and good,
God spake and the water stood
And so shall now the blood.
In the name of the Father, Son and Holy Ghost.   Amen

To cure a scald or burn

The charmer places a hand on the burn and says in a soft voice:

Three angels came from the north, east and west.
One brought fire, another brought ice
And the third brought the Holy Ghost.
So out fire and in frost.
In the name of the Father, Son and Holy Ghost.   Amen

To ensure good sight

Fennel, rose, vervain, celandine and rue,
Do water make which will the sight renew.

To cure zweemy-headedness

Wash the head with plenty of old rum, and the back and face with sour wine. Wear flannel next to the skin and carry a packet of salt in the left-hand pocket.

Charm for a thorn in the flesh

'Our dear Lord Jesus Christ was pricked with thorns. His blood went back to Heaven again, his flesh neither cankered, rankled nor festered, neither shall thine, [name]. In the name of the Father, the Son and the Holy Ghost.   Amen.'

To cure a nose bleed, method 1

Take one or two fine old toads, place them in a baking dish in a cold oven, increase the heat until sufficiently fierce to cook the toads and reduce them to a brown crisp mass. Remove from the oven and beat them to powder in a stone mortar. Place the powder in a box and use as snuff.

To cure a nose bleed, method 2

Say nine times, with absolute faith, these words: 'Blood abide in this vein as Christ abideth in the church, and hide in thee as Christ hideth from himself.'

The bleeding will immediately cease. If, however, you have not shown sufficient faith, take another pinch of toad snuff.

To cure dropsy

Take several large fully-grown toads and proceed as above. Place the ashes in a wide-mouthed jar, cork closely and keep in a dry place. Dosage: one teaspoonful of ashes in milk, to be taken on nine successive mornings while the moon is waxing.

To cure pimples or blackheads

Crawl under a bramble bush clockwise on three successive Sundays; but it must be a bramble which has rooted itself at both ends to form a natural arch.

To cure a corn

Crush a little slug and put it on the smooth side of an ivy leaf; then put it on the corn.

To cure sciatica, or 'boneshave'

Take a pail of clean river water, dipped from a fast-flowing stream, a pair of shears, a large key and a new table knife. Dip the knife into the pail of water, draw it back upwards, downwards, and across the hip, three times each way. Then dip the key into the water and proceed as before. then dip the shears into the water and 'shear' the hip, as though it were covered in wool. Return the water left in the bucket to the river, singing:

As this watter goeth to zay,
So floweth boneshave away.

Seven drops

Medicine should always be taken in odd numbers of drops; seven and nine drop doses are best.

To cure barngun, or ringworm

Barngun is cured by blessing, and the outward application of clotted cream, thus. Take three locks of wool, one white, one grey, one black. Dip them in a basin of clotted cream; when thoroughly saturated, each lock in succession should be rubbed against each infected piece of skin. Hang the wool on sprigs of white thorn to dry in the wind. Repeat this process five, seven or nine times, as the case may require. Whilst lubricating the sores, chant in monotone the following:

'There were three angels come from the west, to cure [name} of the barngun, white barngun, red barngun, black barngun, aching, sticking, pricking barngun, all sorts of barngun, barngun bubee, ill will I prove 'ee. I stick thee up on thees yer thorn, there thou shalt die and never come near'n no more. In the name of the Father, the Son and the Holy Ghost. Amen.'

The potato cure for rheumatism

Take a freshly dug early potato, wash it free of soil, and ask a member of the opposite sex to place it, unobserved by you, in a pocket of one of your garments. Having once worn the garment carrying the tuber, you can yourself change it to another pocket or another garment, but it must be carried continuously, not intermittently, or the charm will be lost. (It is probably safest to wear it at night also.) As the potato hardens, the rheumatism will leave the system.

It was once common for farm labourers to carry a potato in every waistcoat pocket, until they looked like small grey stones, and were equally hard.

To cure whooping cough

Bring an ass before the door of the house, into whose mouth thrust a slice of new bread; then pass the child three times over and under the animal's body, and the charm is completed.

Recording a charm in print

The first time any charm is written down in print, its former effectiveness is totally destroyed. Sorry about that.